BORN IN THE TIME OF CORONA

Written by Dr. Fatima Almutairi

Illustrated by alhyari

For my daughter Reem,
born in April 2020.

Mummy, mummy! Tell me again,
how the world was back then.

Back before I could walk
or run or skip or even talk!

Oh alright my dear,
but again you must know..
this story is not all sweet,
there is grief and sorrow.

Indeed it was a time
of uncertainty and fear.
A new ailment had arrived,
yes, coronavirus was here!

SALE!

It could spread through a cough
or unwashed hands to start.
Everyone had to wear masks
and stand two metres apart.

Sadly it made a lot of people sick
and some more so than others.
Indeed it was a difficult time for all,
from parents to sisters and brothers.

And while most of us were stuck at home
to keep safe and unharmed.
There was a lot to be gained,
so do not be alarmed.

We explored our hidden talents
and learned the value of patience.

While painting or baking,
or just reading in silence.

We tidied our homes
from room to room.

We dusted and polished
and swept with our brooms.

We organised our closets
to donate clothes we had outgrown.

And video called our grandparents
to remind them, they weren't alone.

We gathered around as a family
on the living room floor.

Eating homemade banana bread
and played board games galore.

We also went out for walks
to enjoy some fresh air.
We admired the trees and flowers,
and the big blue sky, up there!

We were also very thankful,
my darling child of mine,
to all the people working
on the frontline.

From doctors and nurses
and police officers too!
All working to keep us safe,
to list just a few.

But above all my dear
it gave us time to reflect.
A new appreciation for life
we will never neglect.

To always be grateful
for our families and health.
For this is indeed
the greatest form of wealth.

So rest your head little one
and never forget..

how beautiful life truly is,
a lesson you won't regret.

SHARE YOUR STORY

With Ted

List of things I did during quarantine:

-
-
-
-

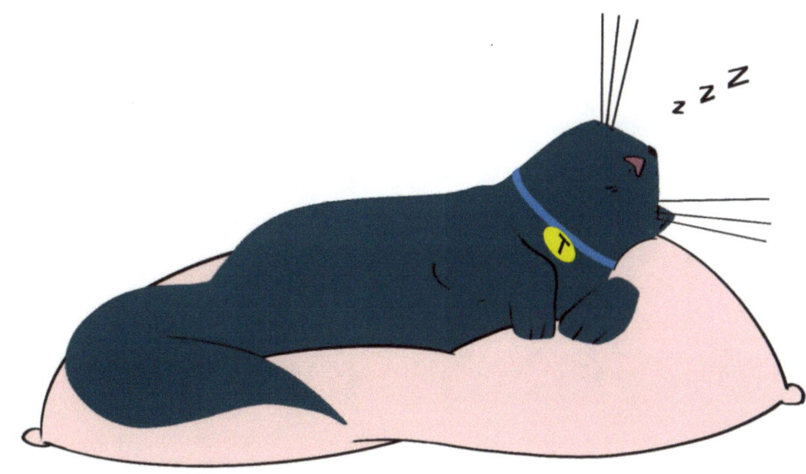

List of things I am grateful for:

-
-
-
-

TED

Draw your hopes for the future:

ONE WAY
Find: